The Energy of Slaves

Books by Leonard Cohen

POETRY

Let Us Compare Mythologies (1956)

The Spice-Box of Earth (1961)

Flowers for Hitler (1964)

Parasites of Heaven (1966)

Selected Poems 1956-1968 (1968)

FICTION

The Favorite Game (1963)

Beautiful Losers (1966)

Leonard Cohen

The Energy of Slaves

The Viking Press / New York

Contents

Welcome to these lines
There is a war on
but I'll try to make you comfortable
Don't follow my conversation
it's just nervousness
Didn't I make love to you
when we were students of the East
Yes the house is different
the village will be taken soon
I've removed whatever
might give comfort to the enemy
We are alone
until the times change
and those who have been betrayed
come back like pilgrims to this moment
when we did not yield
and call the darkness poetry

I threw open the shutters
light fell on this poem
It fell on the name of a man
tortured on a terrace
above a well-known street
I swore by the sunlight
to avenge his broken feet

3

I threw open the shutters:
light fell on these lines
(which are incomplete)
It fell on two words
which I must erase:
name of a man
tortured on a terrace
above a well-known street
I swore by the sunlight
to take his advice:
remove all evidence from my verse
forget about his punctured feet

4

This is the only poem
I can read
I am the only one
can write it
Others seem to think
the past can guide them
My own music
is not merely naked
It is open-legged
It is like a cunt
and like a cunt
must needs be houseproud
I didn't kill myself
when things went wrong
I didn't turn
to drugs or teaching
I tried to sleep
but when I couldn't sleep
I learned to write
I learned to write
what might be read
on nights like this
by one like me

5

All men delight you

If you ever read this
think of the man writing it

he hated the world on your behalf

6

I'd like to read
one of the poems
that drove me into poetry
I can't remember one line
or where to look

The same thing
happened with money
girls and late evenings of talk

Where are the poems
that led me away
from everything I loved

to stand here
naked with the thought of finding thee

7
PORTRAIT OF A GIRL

She sits behind the wooden shutters
on a very hot day
The room is dark, the photographs gloomy
She is profoundly worried
that her thighs are too big
and her ass fat and ugly
Also she is too hairy
The lucky American girls are not hairy
She sweats too much
There is a fine mist caught
on the dark hairs above her mouth
I wish I could show her
what such hair and haunches
do for one like me
Unfortunately I don't know who she is
or where she lives
or if indeed she lives at all
There is no information about this person
except in these lines
and let me make it clear
as far as I'm concerned
she has no problem whatsoever

My skin is made of stars
that tell me what to do.
Turn on the light. I am a dwarf.
You could love me as an embalmed child
if my legs were not so thick and short.

Your confessions of ignorance
charmed me once upon a time.
Teach me to be happy
you said to everyone in bed.
You bought them an expensive
apple if they tried

I am a fastidious dwarf. You thought
I could keep you beautiful
with a lamentation. Even now
you are ready to begin again
but I am too busy washing.

I want to tell my past to a doctor
but I want to tell it to a doctor
who does not love the past
who will not say at last: But remember
you are and you are not a dwarf.

Keep the fire. Keep the fire.
Your body is holy.
Do not believe the truth.
The truth is tiny compared
to the things you have to do.
You are long and thin and fair.

9

There are no traitors among women
Even the mother does not tell the son
they do not wish us well

She cannot be tamed by conversation
Absence is the only weapon
against the supreme arsenal of her body

She reserves a special contempt
for the slaves of beauty
She lets them watch her die

Forgive me, partisans,
I only sing this for the ones
who do not care who wins the war

Poetry begun in this mood rarely succeeds
the girl wasn't at the cafe
the poet has overeaten
in fact he begins this poem
at another café
waiting for his second dinner
we have little hope
        for his art or his evening
He will probably have to
        buy an airplane ticket to Montreal
and sleep one night
with the mistress
        he plans to abandon
I'll get the bill for it all
in the middle of the winter
Since I have introduced myself
let me go on to say
there are perfect heart-shaped leaves
climbing the bamboo trellis
        of this small café
When not admiring them
from the naturalist's point of view
they remind me
of the lights on Broadway
and if this entire small café
became a World War Two fighter plane
these brave green hearts
would be stencilled on the fuselage
instead of
        swastikas and the rising sun

I am invisible to night
Only certain shy women see me
All my hideous days of visibility
I longed for their smiles
Now they lean out of their shabby
plans-for-the-evening
so we may salute one another
Sisters of mine
of my own shattered people
going after third-choice lovers
they smile at me to indicate
that we can never meet
as long as we permit
this order of things to persist
in which we are the wretched ones

It takes a long time to see you Terez
I guess you must be brushing your hair
or touching your forehead to your knee

Take this song and clumsy melody
Keep me waiting in Room 801
like you did that night when we were young

the tomboy in lace and the jockstrapped girl
and with your spirit lover
                    on the cushion of your finger
moan for me
as I will moan for you my love
as I will moan for thee

I did not know
>>> until you walked away
you had the perfect ass
Forgive me
>>> for not falling in love
with your face or your conversation

OVERHEARD ON EVERY CORNER

Sometimes I remember
that I have been chosen
to perfect all men
the fireflies remind me
the stream beside my shack
If I was meant to be a poet
I would not be able to blow
the actual flawless smokerings
for which I am renowned
I would be distracted
by the possible beauty of my pen
but I am not
I would lose myself
I would have lost myself
with the women
I so relentlessly pursued
but I did not
I was meant to be
the seed of your new society
I was meant to be
the courtless invisible king
I am that
the clearest example of royalty
who serves you tonight
as he makes a bed for the dog
and the fireflies burn
at their different heights

Did you ever moan beneath me
Virgin of Amnesia
If you surrendered I forget
and
let me be your bright new toy
I am the first
to wear your shackles like a
bracelet
first spy and traitor
in the Board Room fields

I am no longer at my best practising
the craft of verse
I do better
in the cloakroom with Sara
But even in this alternate realm
I am no longer at my best
I need
the mercy of my own attention
Who could have foretold
the heart grows old
from touching others

I perceived the outline of your breasts
through your Hallowe'en costume
I knew you were falling in love with me
because no other man could perceive
the advance of your bosom into his imagination
It was a rupture of your unusual modesty
for me and me alone
through which you impressed upon my shapeless hunger
the incomparable and final outline of your breasts
like two deep fossil shells
which remained all night long and probably forever

I don't want you to know who I am
I'm eating a juicy orange by lamplight
but that's none of your business now
now that you've got 'Vietnam' and the 'blacks'
and no longer have to think about who
scratched her dress off in the heat
I have no electricity or power
nor is it a foreign claw
that tears this from my first and only heart

19

I know there's no such thing
                as hell or heaven
I know it's 1967
but are you sleeping have you slept
with any of my friends
It's not just something I want to know
it's the only thing I want to know
not about the mystery of God
not about myself
and am I the beautiful one
The only wisdom I want to have
is to know if I am
or if I am not alone in your love

I try to keep in touch wherever I am
I don't say I love you
I don't say I worked it out
The sun comes in the skylight
My work calls to me
sweet as the sound of the creek
beside the cabin in Tennessee
I listen at my desk
and I am almost ready to forgive
the ones who tried to crush us
with their fine systems
Your beauty is everywhere
which we distilled together
out of the hard times

You will never feel me leading you
Forever I escape your homage
I have no ideas to shackle you
I have nothing in mind for you
I have no prayers to put you in
I live for you
without the memory of what you deserve
or what you do not deserve

Your eyes are very strong
They try to cripple me
You put all your strength
into your eyes
because you do not know
how to be a hero

You have mistaken your ideal
It is not a hero
but a tyrant
you long to become
Therefore weakness
is your most attractive quality

I have no plans for you
Your dangerous black eyes
fasten on the nearest girl
or the nearest mirror
as you go hopefully
from profession to profession

It is not to tell you anything
but to live forever
that I write this
It is my greed that you love
I have kept nothing for myself
I have despised every honour
Imperial and mysterious
my greed has made a slave of you

O love
did the world come to you
in the form of a woman
and you
were you training with mirrors
to make yourself perfect

There is no end to my hatred
except in your arms
　　　　Strange as it seems
I am the ghost of Joan of Arc
　　　　and I am bitter bitter
in the consequence of voices
　　　　Hold me tight
or I will have you sweating
where I was

25

I am dying
   because you have not
died for me
   and the world
still loves you

I write this because I know
that your kisses
   are born blind
on the songs that touch you

I don't want a purpose
   in your life
I want to be lost among
            your thoughts
the way you listen to New York City
when you fall asleep

cutting the hair
and other forms of discipline
rituals excluding cunt and wine
I used to act so pretty
when I was looking for a girl
did you notice I'm not
talking to you anymore
you can rest now
this is the most peaceful music in the world

I left a woman waiting
I met her sometime later
she said, Your eyes are dead
What happened to you, lover

And since she spoke the truth to me
I tried to answer truly
Whatever happened to my eyes
happened to your beauty

O go to sleep my faithful wife
I told her rather cruelly
Whatever happened to my eyes
happened to your beauty

I wore a medal of the Virgin
round my throat
I was always a slave
Play with me forever
           Mistress of the World
Keep me hard
Keep me in the kitchen
Keep me out of politics

You are a much finer person than I am
Your poetry is better too
There is always blood on your apple
and only sometimes on mine
I act like a fool
when I speak to two girls on yet another night
the one cunt sunk like an imperial bathtub
in my slippery conversation
and the other an endless tribute to Helen Keller
Choose me louder please
if only in the moment that you fall
We could be lovers begging together

—I don't know what to call it, he said.
—Call it your friend.
—My friend.
She held it, not as tightly as he wanted.
—God, it looks so archaic, she said.

The silly girl, the silly girl, o the silly goose, look
at her gooseflesh!

> She stood up.

As soon as the water was very shallow, she stood up, leaving
the crouch with which she waded

Write with compassion about the deceit in the human heart,
in my heart, about my appetite for revenge, how I hate you
when others love you more than you love me, how I hope
your art will fail, when others love you more than I love
you, when others love you more than they love me, my
unceasing struggle for fame and money, my lies, the lies I
tell you in order to trick and eventually humiliate you,
because this is one of my intentions

From whose point of view are you trying to love your
body, composing special expressions for yourself when you
consult the mirror, concealing your double chin even from
yourself

You can no longer control the ones you love

Are you happy now that no one wants to undress you,
wants to kiss and caress and handle your (you have no
idea what to call it)

And is this what you wanted
      to live in a house that is haunted
by you and me

I make this song for thee
Lord of the World
who has everything in the world
except this song

Listening to her song
I looked out the window
at all the young matadors
cruising the record shops
on Clinton Street

I've lost my pride
I'm not proud any longer
It turned out that
I was only a scribbler
and not the slice of apple
you would cut your wrists upon

There's a lot of music
on Clinton Street
There's some winter now
in every sunny step
Many dancing people
found out about the winter

You heard me begging
I put aside every ornament
of my voice
I heard myself
            forsaking beauty
and shame drove out
the appetite for music

Before I go
I'd like to thank
the singers
in the basement
on their knees confessing

34
SCORPION

O rare and perfect creature
Who has made your nest in me
I'm on my way home to you
singing with the lips
you bloodied out of jealousy
I am your world
I am your wall
You are the last scorpion
Who never longed to be a man
It is only in my heart
that you can dream
of your relentless invasion
of the sunlit plain
when you moved among the numberless
and a woman far more beautiful
than I am
was your invisible queen
Scorpion scorpion
master of the hollow stone
I will not let them crush you
I do not like their reasons
My heart is numb and swollen
from keeping you
in the safety of your anger
I never could foretell
the loyalty that would claim me
They will not wear you on a brooch
they will not watch you
in a paperweight
I am your dominion
I am your exercise

You hate the world I visit
and I am punished
by your solitary truth
Everything you say
about the world is true

Each day he lugged
a hunk of something precious
over to his boredom
and once or twice a week
when he was granted
the tiny grace of distance
he perceived that he laboured
as his fathers did
on someone else's pyramid

Thoughts of rebellion
Thoughts of injustice
New Year's resolutions
The seduction of a woman
All these he engraved
numbly letter by letter

Walther PPK–S
Serial No. 115142
stolen from one slave by another

Stay
    stay a little longer
timid shadow
            of my repose
    fastened so lightly
            to the breath before
                    my first question

Thou art the hunger
can disarm
            every appetite

    What embrace
            satisfies the child
    who will not kill?

If I could tell you
the laws of my longing
you would be here
on behalf of your greed
the witness of a hungry man
who does not care
if you are naked or shy

Because now that I
can't use it or feel it
I know for a fact
that I am beautiful
and more than anything
you want a beautiful slave
to make you cry

And long after that
whenever I touched you
whenever you undressed
you would need to know
what I was thinking
and you would be as treacherous
as you know you are
you would be a spy

And then something would happen
that would crush us
and free us
and destroy completely
whatever had been
we would have begun
to signal one another
each time before we lie

What character could possibly engage my boredom, that exquisite spoiled princess in the palace of my failure? She refuses even to imagine him with whom I must inspire her hopelessness, and she barely speaks to me.

The story is already complicated by my indifference. I believe she longs for a woman.
She does not want the gift to come from me.

She wants to wear delicate men's trousers and live with this woman in a port town where they will perfect sweet rituals such as walking together at twilight smoking cigarillos past shadowy retired fishermen who learn to accept them as another species of bird which they would judge no more fiercely than the seagull or the heron.

I could have created such a woman out of the one or two women who loved me, but in those days I had no taste for monsters, although I must say that they did.

She sat down at the piano
the most beautiful pianist in the world
dressed in a photographer's robe
   I was rambling through the yellow pages
of my old slave's heart
for something better than gratitude
   when upon the mucous she installed
the tiniest royal sailing ship
the sea has ever given back
   saying, Sometimes I am with thee
sometimes I must go to where
a man is stranger to his pain

40
MOROCCO

I bought a man his dinner
He did not wish to look into my eyes
He ate in peace

I was lost
when I met you on the road
to Larissa
the straight road between the cedars

You thought
I was a man of roads
and you loved me for being such a man
I was not such a man

I was lost
when I met you on the road
to Larissa

42

There is no one
to show these poems to
Do not call a friend to witness
what you must do alone
These are my ashes
I do not intend to save you any work
by keeping silent
You are not yet as strong as I am
You believe me
but I do not believe you
This is war
You are here to be destroyed

43
THE PROGRESS OF MY STYLE

I rarely think of you darling
Tonight I indulge myself
remembering the beauty you lost
in your thirtieth year
but I can't get off on it
I have no altar for my song

I'm living with a woman in Montreal
My inspiration failed
I abandoned the great plan
Among other things
I got wiped out
by several charismatic holy men

I wish there was a tree
and a café
with my best friend talking
Thighs from my old poems
would help
None of the items can appear
for political reasons

Perhaps you can detect
that I still try for music
idle music for the very idle
you might say unemployed
working to reach you like a computer
through holes in the paper

44

I dream of torturing you
because you are so puffed up with pride
You stand there with a bill of rights
or an automatic rifle
or your new religion
I am the angel of revenge
The flowers and the mountains
the milky afternoons of childhood
all innocent and abandoned forms
have designated me
the angel of revenge
This machine is rubber and metal
it fits over your body and you die slowly

45

Leaning over his poem
from a standing position
wearing underwear
the bed unmade
the poem half made
he crosses out a line
he stands back
the serious worker
the teen-age craftsman
The poem is found later
in a collection
We are left alone the boy and me
the boy and me are married by my will
they retire unhappily
to the unmade bed
I arrange the divorce
I refrain from comforting you tonight
Treacherous girls hide my songs
under drifts of make-up
Leaving the company of great thieves
I return to my solitary adventure

46
CRYING, COME BACK, HERO

Now we're tough enough again
to speak for love alone,
let politics go hang, we've
had our try with twisted form:
what good was it but training
for a summer day, discipline
to keep our manhood hard and warm.
One man free to love his minute
in the realms of flesh and sun
breaks down more pain than ages
of humane law or lawyers can.
Speaking softly one last time
let me say, You've made your laws
too strong, good or bad, your laws
have weakened many men, and I
would rather haunt cafés on both
sides of town than break my only
heart for your millennium,
my beloved falling through the numbered
arms of weak and weaker men.
It's panic in the eyes of girls
that tells me I must speak for love alone,
panic at their empty beds,
at sanitary rows of monsters born.

1965

47

You provide the furniture
if you want to live here.
Do you like this song?
I wrote it in a mood
that I would never
be seen dead in.
Put your chair
where your mouth is,
and I welcome your opinion

Over there   a little altar
Over there   one city or another
Over there   your miserable 'sex life'
Spare us the details
You hide behind your nakedness
When you are bold enough
you impose it like a bad government

49

One of these days
You will be the object
of the contempt of slaves
Then you will not talk so easily
about our freedom and our love
Then you will refrain
from offering us your solutions
You have many things on your mind
We think only of revenge

BEAUTY SPEAKS IN THE THIRD ACT

And so your purpose failed
you could not hear high music
your mistress fell into a trance
of everyday behaviour
money found an honoured place
at your expanding table
and the city was your home
I moved aside
long before you sent a delegate
to say you could not use me
I left you for another hungry man
who waited for me all his childhood
as once you did yourself
Now I bring you news
of this other one

PICTURE OF THE ARTIST AND HIS ROOM

His first masterpiece, the painterly art
invisible, detail photographic
and accident, our newest rhetoric
bravely absent, except that he had to start
somewhere and it was this room that stopped him
between women: that's all he owes to chance.
He might be waiting for an ambulance,
a naked woman, or the Seraphim
of God. But he's not. He's going to get up
and paint his room at midnight with himself
in the corner saying, This is myself.
This is the bed. This is the plastic cup.
I am one, I am welcome, like the chair,
the table, any of the objects there.

Why is it
  I have nothing to say to you
Russian princess
      in 1920 furs
coming down the steep steps
  careful of the ice
on Ave de l'Esplanade
      You were extremely fragile
in your hold on beauty
and I cared so much
      you wouldn't slip
that I had to kick you
      down the stairs
just to savour
  unemployment once again

53

This is a threat
Do you know what a threat is
I have no private life
You will commit suicide
or become like me

Terez and Deanne elude me
Terez and Deanne
    that is how great a poet I am

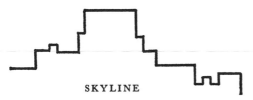

SKYLINE

and artist too
    I could grow to love
the fucking in New York
        far from the soil
but dreamy and courageous

You need her
so you can get
your boots off the bedspread

We who have always ruled the world
don't like the way you dance

And she said, I for one
am happy with the world

She seized the lapel of a cut-throat
and said it again
with all her small voice trembling,
I for one am happy with the world

I don't know if I want to kill her or not

HOW WE USED TO APPROACH
THE BOOK OF CHANGES: 1966

Good father, since I am now broken down, no leader
of the borning world, no saint for those in pain,
no singer, no musician, no master of anything, no
friend to my friends, no lover to those who love me
   only my greed remains to me, biting into every
minute that has not come with my insane triumph
   show me the way now, tonight, to possess what
I long for, to ensnare, to tame, to love and be loved
by —— in the passion which I cannot ignore despite
your teachings
   give her to me and let me be for a moment in
this miserable and bewildering wretchedness, a happy
animal

To the men and women
        who own men and women

those of us meant to be lovers
we will not pardon you
for wasting our bodies and time

58

I sit with the old men
watching you dance
We never found a way
to outwit your husband
I suggested a simple lie
You held out for murder

I buy a yellow pencil
for the sake of innocence
I leave you to your husband
and a Greek marine on leave
who is touching you too much
touching you too much

In my small courtyard
the trees whisper to my soul
I have been in love with them
all my life
their company is sweet
they no longer rule the world

There was a veil between them
composed of good thread
not carelessly woven

therefore they did not ignore it
or poke at it, but honoured
what hid them, one from the other

thus they served their love
as those old Spanish lovers served
The One Who Does Not Manifest Himself

I will grow old
the photograph will age
I will die
the photograph enter a museum
Study the naked ones
they too grew old
even the naked ones
even the abandoned ones
The photograph tells you
the way you hold your cunt
is old-fashioned

61

I dress in black
I have green eyes
              in certain light

If others try to write this
death to them
death to anyone
if he or she unseal this poem
in which I dress in black

and bless your eyes
who hurry from this page
Put a green-eyed man
out of his misery and rage

62

I walk through the old yellow sunlight
to get to my kitchen table
the poem about me
lying there with the books
in which I am listed
among the dead and future Dylans

You can understand
I am in no hurry to make the passage
The sunlight is old and yellow
a flood of what I laboured
to distill a tiny drop of
in that shabby little laboratory
called my talent

I stand here dreaming in my sweat
(you would fall in love with me again)
dreaming of a tie a shirt
a white suit a life
a new life in a warm city
far from the envious practice
of written speech

O look what the summer
has done to the daisies in my yard
Their skeletons must look like scrap and junk
to many lovers of the cabbage
(and to be perfectly fair
even to many lovers of the daisy)

Dance on the money
the heads of presidents
red toenails

this 'poem' is an I.O.U.
for 10,000 drachmas
on your step-smooth shoulders

My table rushes up
to give you a marble stage
black olives live forever
in the tired oil of your grace

Sinking under needles of bazouki
you threaten us with jobs in the Sahara
or a salary of halvah
        oh the hair is real
that pilots the thighs
into the important satin theatre
ruined like Greece by overuse
but all we have of the Golden age

Your courting clothes sleeping in cedar
your grandmother still alive on Hydra
'Don't tell her that you saw me naked'

I have been cruel to you
but that was when I was thin
a fugitive from employment
in your dressing room
        a critic of your veils
and the stars on your nipples
'Every man considers himself a connoisseur
of Belly Dancing'

        I join the jealous applause of kings
each one at his lonely table
with its white saucer satellite of American money
there to honour you
remembering our time last week
when slavery peeled from the world
like an old snakeskin
as we emerged
through the back door of the café
into an alley off 8th Avenue
hand in hand
drunk and silent among the cold morning clouds
as we moved toward our marriage
in the unwritten history of New York

Perhaps it is because my music
does not sing for me

I hate my music
I long for weapons

Some men find strength
by going their lonely ways
let us be what we can to them

The sea-lions live a wonderful life
I wish we could leave them alone
They will cause us to make love in rubber suits
It has been said
that I am not the leader of my generation
There is ample evidence
Not only is the dog friendly
he believes he is human
My case is similar
I want to be left alone
in your great envious heart

The Ark you're building
in your yard
Will you let me on
Will you let me off
Don't you think
we all should study Etiquette
before we study Magic

N.Y. 1967

What has taken place in your body and your head
that allows you to address yourself like this
Surely you know
And if you do not know
as obviously you do not know
how can I destroy the wretch who does not love you

N.Y. 1967

I let your mind enter me
out of loneliness
I was a house for your vision
but I cannot do this twice
Don't walk on your shadow
Don't step on my broom
I will keep your shadow clean

N.Y. 1967

Welcome home
resume your kingdom
the girls have forgotten you
Marianne will remain
a beautiful and mysterious name
whenever you see it written down
Come in now
all the curious landscapes
which you surrendered
are still your own
you could not trade them
for priesthood or gold or revolution
Walk down eighth avenue with me
ask anyone for a cigarette

N.Y. 1967

I could not wait for you
to find me dead in a rented room
with my sunglasses dusty
                    on the card table
So once again
I tried to set my throat on fire
this time in silence
and not thinking of you at all
(I had so much time to kill)

They locked up a man
who wanted to rule the world
The fools
They locked up the wrong man

You are almost always with someone else
I'm going to burn down your house
and fuck you in the ass
If you have the presence of mind
to look over your shoulder
you'll see me swooning
Why don't you come over to my table
with no pants on
I'm sick of surprising you.

73

Dipped myself in a future night
like a long-armed candle-maker
Came back too gross for love
Useless as I seem in my coat of greed
I will have an unborn woman
when I am only print

Come down to my room
I was thinking about you
and I made a pass at myself

Valentina gave me four months
of her twentieth year
and then returned to a rich man
who lived in the Plaza Hotel

She watched television all day long
and she never told me a lie
I loved to creep up behind her
when she was engrossed in Star Trek
and kiss her little ass-hole

It was a happy hotel room at the Chelsea
We never let anyone come over
(I do not think she minded my pranks)

I have a sneer for you
I deliver it to the lapels of my overcoat
but it belongs to you
One of these days
I'm going to try to stop them
from killing you
but it will be reluctantly
   In my speech to the jury
I will remember if I can
the fragrance of your skin
   perhaps you can get away
with five years People's Field Whore

It gets dark at four o'clock now
The windshield is filled with night and cold
the motor running for the heater's sake
We finally forgive ourselves
and touch each other between the legs
At last I can feel the element of welcome in our kisses

It was a while ago
when I was still smoking cigarettes
when I left women waiting
and shopped at Le Château
when I was still
the sweetest singer I could imagine
It's too dark in here
the light isn't any good
And stop asking me questions
nobody's gonna notice
if I never write again
except that incredible
natural blonde over there
that all the boys are fighting over
them roses are dangerous

79

You tore your shirt
to show me where
you had been hurt
I had to stare

I put my hand
on what I saw
I drew it back
It was a claw

Your skin is cured
You sew your shirt
You throw me food
and change my dirt

You want me at all times
without my prophet's mantle
without my loneliness
without the jelly girls
You want me without my agony
without the risk
        that my health insults you
without my love of trees
without my ocean hut
You want me to lose the thread
        in my friend's conversation
without my memory
without my promise to animals
and come here and come here
and come here and come here
and come here and come here
and come here and come here
and come here and come here
and come here and come here
and come here and come here
and come here and come here

Why did you spend
another night with her
when you could have slept
with Naked Jane
or bought yourself
a twelve-year oriental girl
Why don't they make Vietnam
worth fighting for

It is a trust to me
most holy out of my day
deeper than black opium
    that travelled me out of my lessons
louder than the firereels of Cuba
    where I did not kill the man

It is a trust
and when I find it
(losing it losing it often)
I am a banner alone
I am a wise soldier
I walk with my mouth shut
into the drifting world
gripped by the honour

Havana 1961

he whistled to himself
in the millionaire's living-room
he said something romantic to himself
about a blonde girl of war and the iron rain
he smoked a cigarette
and stubbed it in a marble ashtray
he didn't steal anything
he left the news of a thief
he said something romantic to himself
about his solitary occupation
as he climbed down the outside
of the black Manhattan skyscraper
the people will come back
from the charity ball
and never feel at home again

His suicide was simply not a puzzle
even to those of us
who photographed him
with his mouth open
behind a grime of dots

We saw him meeting a girl
quite by accident
the blue night of the estate
upheld by lemon trees
resembling small-faced orchestras

We stood by on the rim
of a bullet hole looking down
as he laced her huge new boot
with a boa constrictor

Sing for him, Leonard,
your love of honey qualifies you
to wear his raincoat
and his stinging shaving lotion
for this purest of occasions

I am punished when I do not work on this poem
or when I try to invent something
I am one of the slaves
You are employees
That is why I hate your work

Perhaps she would come again
perhaps she would come for the first time
perhaps it was the girl
who entered without knocking
and saw in the courtyard a man
whose genitals were sparkling in the sunlight
with the semen of self-love
and stared long before she fled.
Let there be a Law that says
she owes him one, one vision of herself to crack
to smash to utterly disgrace
the fortress plastercast of beauty
that keeps her from him
that keeps her in the song of other men

the 15-year-old girls
I wanted when I was 15
I have them now
it is very pleasant
it is never too late
I advise you all
to become rich and famous

ON HEARING THAT IRVING LAYTON
WAS KISSED BY ALLEN GINSBERG
AT A TORONTO POETRY READING

Not to alarm you Irving
but I have it
from a friend of
the deceased Irish poet
that soon after
he received
          the blessings of
Allen Ginsberg
Patrick Kavanagh died

The poet is drunk
He wonders what
he will write next
He has some notion of poetry
girl's names and ages
the weather in cities
that's about it
Now comes the miracle
his absolute privacy
violates itself before our eyes
his absolute privacy
forbids the violation
Three nights at the Hilton
a girl with round buttocks
suntanned and cheerful, fourteen, Athens

We call it sunlight
or the dove
or a two twenty-two

It is my language
my cunt   my slave

your advice!
your manifestos!
the next hustle
now that psychiatry
has been disgraced

we call it 'getting a tan'
we call it
        'the British are coming'
many names to match the amplitude
of your ugliness

no instructions come
on how to read this
you would have to be
more beautiful than your father
and your mother
and you aren't

War is no longer needed
to teach you
about torture and pain

Therefore don't congratulate yourself
when the boys come home
Your party did not win

It's the old arrangement
the old party
the one that deals in slavery

The killers that run
        the other countries
are trying to get us
to overthrow the killers
        that run our own
I for one
prefer the rule
        of our native killers
I am convinced
        the foreign killer
will kill more of us
than the old familiar killer does
        Frankly I don't believe
anyone out there
really wants us to solve
our social problems
        I base this all on how I feel
about the man next door
I just hope he doesn't
        get any uglier
Therefore I am a patriot
I don't like to see
        a burning flag
because it excites
the killers on either side
to unfortunate excess
which goes on gaily
        quite unchecked
until everyone is dead

93

Dear Mailer
don't ever fuck with me
or come up to me
and punch my gut
on behalf of one of your theories
I am armed and mad
Should I suffer
the smallest humiliation
at your hand
I will k--l you
and your entire family

94
ON LEAVING FRANCE

the blue sky
makes the plane go slow

they say I stole their money
which is true

let the proprietors of the revolution
consider this:

a song the people loved
was written by a thief

95

Love is a fire
It burns everyone
It disfigures everyone
It is the world's excuse
for being ugly

Whenever I happen to see you
I forget for a while
that I am ugly in my own eyes
for not winning you

I wanted you to choose me
over all the men you know
   because I am destroyed
in their company

I have often prayed for you
like this
   Let me have her

The form of poetry
has been disgraced by many pious hands
That's why I can't write it anymore
I couldn't take the company

Just a while ago
I rejoiced in the imagination
but then I got to thinking

how few girls I know in Montreal
That makes it hopeless

I blame it on me and Suzanne
the death of poetry
and the fucking torture that preceded it

The whole world told me
to shut up and go home
and Suzanne took me down
to her place by the river

There's nothing like starvation
It has even caused high-minded persons
who wish to be known as poets
to stand up and speak out against free love
dressing up for the occasion
in the clothes of honest men

We have earned the hatred of honest men
We no longer merit their indifference
The women were the first to know

You who knew very well you could fuck anyone
but couldn't think of a beautiful way to put it
you'll look fine with your throat cut

98
SONG FOR MY ASSASSIN

We were chosen, we were chosen
miles and miles apart:
I to love your kingdom
you to love my heart.

The love is intermittent
the discipline continues:
I work on your spirit
you work on my sinews.

I watch myself from where you are:
do not be mistaken:
the spider web you see me through
is the view I've always taken.

Begin the ceremony now
that we have been preparing:
I'm tired of this marble floor
that we have both been sharing.

99

I don't know what happens
to you anymore
    the Bible poisoned my love
A drunk goes by the window
I wish
    that I could sing like that
The Bible poisoned my love
and many biographies
    haven't made things easy
Tell me who to kill
tell me who to kill
    cries the slave in my heart
to anyone still standing

I can't believe
              what they say is true
that you didn't shelter the poor
that you didn't
              stand up for the weak
Is it true
is it true
that you did not shelter the poor
and is it true
              in your deepest heart
you thought you were better
Now what can you do
              what can you do
for this crime against love
You must
              give us your blessing
you must
              give us your power

O darling (as we used to say)
you are wide-hipped and kind
I'm glad we ran off together
We are not exactly young
but there is still some pleasure
to be squeezed from these leather bags
Even as we lie here in Acapulco
not quite in each others' arms
several young monks walk single-file
through the snow on Mount Baldy
shivering and farting in the moonlight:
there are passages in their meditation
that treat our love and wish us well

I have no talent left
I can't write a poem anymore
You can call me Len or Lennie now
like you always wanted
I guess I should pack it up
but habits persist
and women keep driving me back into it
Before you accuse me of boring you
(your ultimate triumph and relief)
remember that neither you or me
is fucking right now
and once again you have enjoyed
the company of my soul

This is my voice
but I am only whispering
The amazing vulgarity
of your style
invites men to think
of torturing you to death
but I am only whispering
The ocean is whispering
The junk-yard is whispering
We no longer wish to learn
what you know how to do
There is no envy left
If you understood this
you would begin to shiver
but I am only whispering
to my tomahawk
so that the image itself
may reduce you to scorn
and weaken you further

How we loved you
our first poet
who never knew what he was doing
stumbling and swinging
to embrace the pillars
of the geodesic dome
and bring it down
on drunk and clever guests
We loved your darkest days
in delayed airports
as you laboured to abstract
the beauty of female fellow travellers
willing at last to be ravished
by certain Muzak adaptations
The slow poem was everything
It grew minutely
like rust and wrinkle
on the betrayed covenant
You were tentimes faithless
to every body but this one
bored and dying
whenever you turned
your useless kisses to depend
upon the shades of home
But then it was broken
then it was old
you came back from your dead warm bed
the rainbow veteran
to denounce the gold
to take my hand out of the fire
in my pocket
Welcome to this book of slaves
which I wrote during your exile

you lucky son-of-a-bitch
while I had to contend
with all the flabby liars
of the Aquarian Age

This is the poem we have been waiting for
n'est-ce pas
Much returns to us when we read it
which we do over and over again
It is not inspired
It took days and days to write
You are a detail in it
then you are the engine of the song
If only your gorilla was dead
we could be lovers
You cannot accuse my poem of helping anyone
You cannot use the tone
for the construction of a new thing
We like to read it slowly
touching ourselves
while falling asleep in the charcoal tower
after the terrible goodbye
We stop here and there
to put up red curtains or change the cats
but we come back
filled with sweet gratitude
O sweet gratitude
to be the ones we are
drivers of cars in the night-time rain
toward the adult restaurants and the toughest of lives
in Nashville and Acapulco

The poems don't love us anymore
they don't want to love us
they don't want to be poems
Do not summon us, they say
We can't help you any longer

There's no more fishing
in the Big Hearted River
Leave us alone
We are becoming something new

They have gone back into the world
to be with the ones
who labour with their total bodies
who have no plans for the world
They never were entertainers

I live on a river in Miami
under conditions I cannot describe
I see them sometimes
half-rotted half-born
surrounding a muscle
like a rolled-up sleeve
lying down in their jelly
to make love with the tooth of a saw

Layton was wrong
about the war
He was right
about beauty and death
but he was wrong
about the war
I saw him sleeping
beside Niagara Falls
I don't think he's
going to apologize

I think it is safe to tell you where I
am. I'm writing at the old kitchen table
listening to Bach, looking at the sky
and then down at this page where the fable
of this morning will be quickened by those
tiny gods of unemployment who guide
my curious career, who decompose
my song before my eyes, my leap of pride.
So I see it is not safe at all.
I am not sitting at the old table.
I did not come home. I am not fair and tall.
Bach said he'd play but he was unable
to leave the woman sleeping in his bed
who fleshes out the tunes he'd lose instead.

For a long time
    he had no music
    he had no scenery

He killed three people
    in the darkness of his greed
The rain could not help him

Pass by
    this is no vision offered
this is his truth

Any system you contrive without us
will be brought down
We warned you before
and nothing that you built has stood
Hear it as you lean over your blueprint
Hear it as you roll up your sleeve
Hear it once again
Any system you contrive without us
will be brought down
You have your drugs
You have your guns
You have your Pyramids your Pentagons
With all your grass and bullets
you cannot hunt us any more
All that we disclose of ourselves forever
is this warning
Nothing that you built has stood
Any system you contrive without us
will be brought down

Each man
has a way to betray
the revolution
This is mine

One of the lizards
was blowing bubbles
as it did pushups on the tree trunk
I did pushups this morning
on the carpet
and I blew bubbles of Bazooka
last night in the car
I believe the mystics are right
when they say we are all One

You went to work at the U.N.
and you became a spy
for a South American government
because you cared for nothing
and you spoke Spanish
That was several years after we made love
in the honey air of autumn Montreal:
Athens was beautiful in the old days
the drug-stores were free
We knew ten great cities by heart
Death to the Powers
who have destroyed the style of travel
Let them stutter their bland secrets
over your long legs and tall fingers
Let them have your wooden love
Death to the Vanguard
Death to the Junta
Death to the Passport Control

Every time my wife has a baby
she goes crazy
she sees the world clearly
and she goes crazy
We have to put her away
so we can get back to the war
Men and women are killed
right in front of the baby

I see the ocean from my window
it is very dull
no whales today
no tidal wave
The fisherman fiddles
with his air conditioner
The sunset is slowly squashed
by the huge forces of night
I telephone my wife
We watch it in each other's arms

There is nothing here
except the shadow
of an occasional DC-3
nobody wants to be on

A Nazi war criminal
visited us last night
a very old man
in a silk parachute

We still love beauty
which the lizards express for us
Spinnakers of red membrane
blow from their throats

We'd like to write more often
but we are busy with the disciplines
psychic self-defence
and other martial arts

We have abandoned free love
and we have established the capital penalty
for certain crimes
There is no longer static between men and women

Our hospitality is simple and formal
we use no intoxicants
We salute those who come and go
We are naked with our friends